MW01230349

AUTHENTIC BAHAMIAN CUISINE

Young Chef Christopher Knowles Presents
The Best Recipes Of The Bahamas

Authentic Bahamian Cuisine Copyright © 2021 by Christopher Knowles. All rights reserved. Printed in the United State of America. No part of this book may be used or reproduced in any manner, whatsoever without written permission.

Contents

Appetizers

Conch salad

Conch salad

Ingredients

- ½ cup tomato (diced)
- ½ cup green bell pepper (diced)
- ¼ cup onion (chopped)
- 2 conchs
- Salt to taste
- Juice of 2 juicy limes
- Juice of ½ juicy orange
- ½ Scotch bonnet pepper or goat pepper

Instructions

1. Prepare the conchs by chopping them into fine pieces—place in a large bowl.
2. Chop the fresh produce and place them into the bowl.
3. Use either a quarter or half of the bonnet pepper or goat pepper to taste.
4. Squeeze the juice from the oranges and limes.
5. Distribute the liquid evenly over the salad.
6. Then season liberally with salt to taste.
7. Mix and serve immediately.

Ready in about: 15 minutes, Servings: 5

Lobster Salad

Lobster Salad

Ingredients

- 2 tbsp. lemon juice
- ¼ cup mayonnaise
- 1 tsp. sugar
- 1 tsp. black pepper
- 1 medium-size onion, finely chopped
- ½ of sweet pepper, finely chopped
- 1 stalk of celery (diced)
- 2 tbsp. chives (chopped)
- 12 oz. lobster tail (steamed and chopped finely)
- 3 tbsp. raisin
- Salt to taste

For servings:
- Avocado sliced
- Lettuce

Instructions

1. In a bowl, combine mayonnaise, celery, onion, sweet pepper, raisin, sugar, black pepper, lemon juice, and chive.
2. Season with salt.
3. Fold in the chopped lobster.
4. On a serving tray, arrange lettuce and then top with lobster salad.
5. Place avocado to garnish.
6. Chill the salad tray in the refrigerator for an hour.
7. Serve and enjoy.

Ready in about: 20 minutes, Servings: 4

Conch Fritters

Conch Fritters

Ingredients

- ¾ cup onion (chopped)
- ½ cup celery (chopped)
- 1 pound conch
- 1 green bell pepper
- 1 tsp. baking powder
- 1½ cups all-purpose flour
- 1 tsp. paprika
- 1 tsp. Salt
- ½ tsp. black pepper
- 1 tsp. dried thyme
- ½ cup milk or water
- 1 scotch bonnet pepper, seedless
- 1-quart vegetable oil for frying

Sauce:
- ¼ cup mayonnaise
- 2 tbsp ketchup
- Hot sauce to taste
- ½ tsp Worcestershire sauce

Instructions

1. Preheat a large pot over medium heat. Add the oil and heat until the temperature reaches 360 degrees Fahrenheit.
2. Cut the conch into smaller pieces and place it into a food processor. Pulse many times to slice into small pieces. Add the bell pepper, onion, celery, and scotch bonnet pepper at this point. Blend to chop finely.
3. Add the conch mixture to a bowl, then add the flour, baking powder, thyme, salt, black pepper, and paprika and whisk until combined thoroughly. Finally, incorporate the milk or water to form a dense batter.
4. Once the oil is hot, separate the batter into balls using a 1/2 tablespoon scoop. Drop the balls gently into the heated oil. Scoop and cook eight to ten fritters at a time, occasionally turning until light brown (for around 4-5 minutes).
5. Arrange paper towels to drain the fried conch fritters. Once the first batch is ready, transfer them to the prepared plate using a skimmer.
6. Cut one open to check if it is fully cooked but still moist. Repeat in 4-5 batches with the remaining batter.
7. To prepare sauce, mix all the ingredients and then serve with the fritters.

Ready in about: 35 minutes, Servings: 40 fritters

Grouper Fingers

Grouper Fingers

Ingredients

- Oil for frying
- 1 egg
- 2 lbs. fresh grouper fillets
- 1 cup flour
- 2 limes
- ¼ cup milk
- Salt and black pepper to taste

Instructions

1. Cut the grouper fillets in strips—season to taste with salt and pepper. Squeeze the lime juice over the fish and marinate for 30 minutes.
2. Add the egg and milk to a bowl and beat until well combined.
3. Preheat oil to 360 degrees F in a saucepan or fryer.
4. Coat the fish with the egg mixture and then dip in the flour.
5. Remove excess flour and cook, occasionally turning until golden brown.
6. Avoid overcrowding the pan.
7. Serve with either the sauce from the conch fritter or with peas and rice.

Ready in about: 55 minutes, Servings: 4

Soups

Conch Chowder

Conch Chowder

Ingredients

- 1 medium onion (chopped)
- 1 medium green pepper (chopped)
- 2 medium carrots (chopped finely)
- 4 potatoes (diced)
- 2 stalks celery (chopped)
- 2 garlic cloves
- 2 bay leaves
- Salt and pepper to taste
- Hot pepper sauce
- 3 tbsp. fresh basil
- 2 tbsp tomato paste
- 2 tbsp. cooking oil
- 10 oz. tomato puree
- 4 conchs chopped

Instructions

1. Boil the conchs in a pot over high heat for 20 minutes, drain, and reserve.
2. Set a large skillet over medium-high heat.
3. Place the oil in the pot and cook until the onion, celery, bell pepper, carrots, and garlic are tender.
4. Combine the drained conchs, potatoes, tomato paste, tomato puree, bay leaves, basil, and hot pepper sauce in a soup pot.
5. Transfer the cooked vegetables to this pot and add enough water to cover.
6. Bring soup pot to a boil over high heat.
7. Reduce to low heat and continue cooking for 1 hour or until the conchs are tender and the potatoes are cooked.
8. Season to taste with salt and pepper.

Ready in about: 1 Hour 30 minutes, Servings: 6

Peas Soup and Dumpling

Peas Soup and Dumpling

Ingredients

- 2 potatoes (diced)
- 2 tbsp. dried thyme
- 1-15 oz can chopped tomatoes
- 1 tbsp. vegetable oil
- 1 lb. pork ribs (chopped)
- 2 onions (chopped)
- 1 green bell pepper
- 2 tbsp tomato paste
- 1 cup smoked ham
- 2-15 oz. can pigeon peas
- Salt and pepper to taste

For dumpling:
- 1 tsp. Salt
- 1 cup white flour
- 1 tsp. baking powder

Instructions

1. Boil the pork ribs for 10 minutes, drain, then rinse thoroughly with water. Combine the pork ribs, cured ham, and pigeon peas in a large pot and cover with enough water. Bring to a boil, then reduce to low heat and partially cover and cook for 30 minutes. Once the meat is cooked, drain and keep aside the broth.
2. Put the meat and pigeon peas back in the pot with the vegetable oil and cook, occasionally stirring, until gently browned. Then add the onions, tomatoes, tomato paste, green bell peppers, thyme, and season with salt and pepper. Simmer for 10 minutes.
3. Reintroduce the strained stock to the pot and continue cooking the soup while preparing the dumplings. Mix the flour, salt, and baking powder with just enough water to form a dough in a bowl.
4. Take 1-inch pieces of dough and roll between your hands, then drop into the soup. Bring to a boil for 10 minutes, then cover, lower to low heat, and continue to cook for another 10 minutes. Remove from heat and set aside for 15 minutes before serving in bowls with local hot pepper sauce and season to taste.

Ready in about: 1 hour 30 minutes, Servings: 4

Crab Soup

Crab Soup

Ingredients

- 6 crabs
- 2 stalks celery (chopped)
- ½ sweet pepper (diced)
- 1 onion (diced)
- 2 tsp oil
- 1 tsp thyme
- 3 tbsp. flour
- Salt and pepper to taste
- 2 cans of coconut milk
- 2 tbsp. tomato paste
- 1/2 medium cabbage (chopped)
- 2 medium carrots (chopped)
- 1 large sweet potato (diced into chunks)
- 2 cups ham (cut into pieces)
- 1 can pigeon peas

Instructions

1. Remove the crab's back (upper) shell. Remove fat from the back shell with care to avoid breaking the bitter gall.
2. Remove the gall and back shells. Remove any excess fat from the body shell. Clean and wash the crabs and crack the claws and body into pieces.
3. Fry the fat and the cleaned crabs and claws until dry.
4. Add the oil to the pot along with the onion, celery, sweet pepper, and thyme. Cook for five minutes and then add the tomato paste and flour and cook for two minutes.
5. Cook stirring continuously until the onions are golden brown.
6. Add the cabbage, sweet potatoes, carrots, ham, pigeon peas, coconut milk, and water to cover the ingredients. Add salt and pepper to taste. Bring to a boil and then reduce heat to low and simmer for 1 hour or until vegetables are cooked.
7. Serve immediately.

Ready in about:1 hour 30 minutes, Servings: 6

Breakfast Recipes

Tuna And Grits

Tuna And Grits

Ingredients

For tuna salad:
- 2 cans of tuna
- 1 lemon - juiced
- ½ yellow onion (chopped finely)
- 1/3 scotch bonnet pepper (chopped finely)
- Salt to taste
- 4 tbsp. mayonnaise

For grits:
- 3 cups water
- 1 egg
- 1 tbsp. butter
- 1 cup yellow grits
- Salt to taste

Instructions

1. Open the tuna cans, drain and place the tuna in a bowl and flake them apart using a fork. Stir in the mayonnaise until combined, and then add the pepper and onion.
2. Season with salt according to your taste, and add lemon juice.
3. Set aside the tuna salad and begin preparing the grits. Because the grits require considerable time and attention to ensure it's not lumpy, I do not recommend cooking them concurrently with the tuna.
4. Bring three cups of water to a boil, then add 1 cup of grits and 1 tbsp butter.
5. Regularly stir until the grits begin to thicken.
6. Crack an egg and add to the mixture. Continue stirring the grits regularly until they have completely absorbed the water. Add salt to taste.
7. The whole procedure should take 20 minutes.
8. Transfer the meal to the serving dish; serve and enjoy.

Ready in about: 30 minutes, Servings: 4

Stewed Fish

Stewed Fish

Ingredients

- 1 small onion (diced)
- 1/3 cup oil
- 2 tsp thyme
- ¾ cup flour
- Salt and pepper to taste
- Juice of 2 limes
- 2-3 lbs. fish (cleaned)
- 2 bay leaves
- 6 cups water
- Oil for frying
- ½ Sweet pepper

Instructions

1. Season the fish with salt and pepper.
2. Squeeze the lime juice over it and marinate for half an hour.
3. Set the pan over medium heat; add some oil and fry the fish in small batches until brown on both sides. Set aside.
4. Set the big saucepan over medium heat, and heat the 1/3 cup of oil.
5. Add the flour and constantly stir until brown.
6. Ensure that it does not burn.
7. Now add in the onion and thyme, and saute for several minutes until tender.
8. Now add boiling water (about 6 cups), the fish, and 2 bay leaves.
9. Reduce to low heat and leave it to simmer for around 15–20 minutes, or until the fish is cooked thoroughly.
10. Serve and enjoy.

Ready in about: 55 minutes, Servings: 3

Boiled Fish

Boiled Fish

Ingredients

- 1 lb. potatoes
- 1 medium onion
- 2 lbs. fish
- 3 tbsp. cooking oil
- Juice of 4 limes
- Water
- Salt to taste
- 3 tsp. of salt and finely crushed bird pepper mix
- 1 hot pepper (chopped)
- ½ celery (chopped)

Instructions

1. Cut fish into large slices—season with the salt and crushed bird pepper mix.
2. Squeeze the juice of 2 limes over it and let marinate for half an hour.
3. Slice the onion into rings and potatoes into 3/8-inch slices.
4. Layer the fish, potatoes, hot pepper, celery, and onions in the same pot.
5. Season the mixture with salt to taste.
6. Add water to the pot to completely cover the potatoes.
7. Add the juice of 2 additional limes.
8. Bring to a low boil, cover, and simmer for about 15-20 minutes until potatoes are tender but still a bit solid.

Ready in about: 40 minutes, Servings: 6

Chicken Souse

Chicken Souse

Ingredients

- 1 tbsp. oil
- 1 large onion (chopped)
- ½ green pepper (chopped)
- 24 chicken wings or 3 lbs -chicken (chopped)
- 3 tbsp. lime juice
- 3 carrots (chopped)
- 2 bay leaves
- 6 large potatoes (diced)
- 2 tbsp. whole allspice
- ¾ cup lime juice
- Salt and pepper to taste
- water
- ½ tsp. red pepper flakes

Instructions

1. Parboil the chicken for ten minutes, then discard the water and wash thoroughly.
2. Combine the chicken, 3 tablespoons lime juice, and salt to taste in a large mixing bowl. Set aside for an hour to marinate at room temperature.
3. Heat the vegetable oil in a large pot over medium heat.
4. Stir the onion and green pepper until the onion has softened and started to brown.
5. Add the potatoes, carrots, red pepper flakes, allspice, bay leaves, marinated chicken, lime juice, and water to cover the ingredients.
6. Bring to a boil, then lower to medium-low heat, cover, and cook until the chicken is no longer pink at the bone.
7. After around 20 minutes, the veggies should be soft.
8. Season with salt and pepper to taste.

Ready in about: 1 hour 30 minutes, Servings: 4

Pig Feet Souse

Pig Feet Souse

Ingredients

- 5 lbs pig feet
- 2.5 lbs pork chop ends
- 2.5 lbs pork rib
- Salt to taste (1 tbsp)
- 2 bay leaves
- 1 tbsp whole allspice
- 5 large limes for juice
- 1 large onion finely chopped
- 1 goat pepper or hot pepper of choice
- Chopped parsley for garnish

Instructions

1. Parboil pigs feet for ten minutes and parboil ribs and chops for five minutes.
2. Pour off the water and rinse in fresh water 5 times or until the water is clear.
3. Combine all the meat in a big pot, and add chopped onion, bay leaves, allspice, salt, lime juice, and pepper.
4. Add water to almost cover the meat and bring to a boil.
5. Reduce heat and boil slowly for an hour or until the meat is soft.
6. Season with salt and pepper if more is needed.
7. Transfer the souse to the serving bowls, garnish with parsley and enjoy.
8. Refrigerate the leftovers as it often tastes better 2 days later.

Ready in about: 1 hour 15 minutes, Servings: 10

Johnny Cake

Johnny Cake

Ingredients

- ½ cup milk
- 1/3 cup water
- 2 cups flour
- ½ cup vegetable oil
- Cooking spray to grease
- ½ tsp. salt
- 3 tsp. baking powder
- 1/3 cup sugar

Instructions

1. Preheat oven to 350 degrees Fahrenheit.
2. Grease the baking pan with cooking spray.
3. Add the flour, salt, and baking powder to a medium bowl.
4. Next, put the sugar, oil, and milk into the mixing bowl.
5. Pour the batter into the assembled baking pan.
6. Bake until lightly golden or until a fork/toothpick inserted in the centre comes out clean.

Ready in about: 30 minutes, Servings: 3

Lunch & Dinner Recipes

Crab & Rice

Crab & Rice

Ingredients

- 6 crabs
- 2 tbsp. cooking oil
- 1 white onion, chopped
- 2 celery stalks, chopped
- ½ green bell pepper, chopped
- 2 tbsp fresh thyme
- Salt and black pepper to taste
- 2 bay leaves
- 2 cloves garlic, mashed
- ½ goat pepper, diced
- 2 tbsp tomato paste
- 1 can diced tomatoes
- 4 cups water
- 1 cup pre-cooked pigeon peas
- 2 cups long-grain rice

Instructions

Preparing the Crabs:
1. Rinse the crabs thoroughly under running water and clean with a toothbrush. Turn each crab over so that the underbelly is facing up. Split the shell in half with a butter knife by pushing upward at the seam.
2. Scoop the fat (orange-brown) off both sides of the shell into a basin using a spoon. Remove the empty half shell, mouth, gills, and any other internal organs that remain.
3. By snapping each segment or chopping with a cleaver, separate each toe and claw at the joint.

Making the Rice:
4. Set the large saucepan over medium-high heat, and heat the cooking oil and crab fat. Once the oil is hot and the fat melts entirely, add the crab, onions, green bell pepper, celery, thyme, salt, black pepper, bay leaves, garlic, and goat pepper; sauté for 3 minutes until the onion is tender.
5. Add the tomato paste and diced tomatoes and cook for an additional 5 minutes. Stir in the water and bring to a boil. Once the water is boiling, add the pigeon peas and rice to the pot and stir to spread evenly.
6. Cover with a tight lid and reduce to low heat; cook for 20-25 minutes, or until the ingredients are tender. While cooking, do not open the cover, as steam must remain in the saucepan to adequately cook the crab.
7. After 25 minutes, remove the pot from the heat. Keep it covered for 10-15 minutes or until all the liquid is absorbed. Serve immediately and enjoy!

Ready in about: 1 hour, Servings: 6

Peas and Rice

Peas and Rice

Ingredients

- 1 small onion, diced
- 1 small sweet pepper, diced
- 1 tbsp. cooking oil
- 2 tbsp. tomato paste
- 4 sprigs of fresh thyme
- Salt and pepper to taste
- 1 tsp. browning (optional)
- 1 fresh tomato, chopped (optional)
- 1 large can of regular pigeon peas
- 2 cups long-grain white rice (approximately)
- 3 cups water

Instructions

1. Heat the oil and sauté the onion, sweet pepper, and thyme in a heavy-bottomed saucepan.
2. Add tomato paste and (optional browning and chopped tomato).
3. Stir in the pigeon peas and 3 cups water.
4. Bring to a boil—season with salt and pepper to taste.
5. Add rice until it reaches a depth of approximately an inch and a half below the waterline.
6. Decrease the heat to medium-low and leave the pot uncovered.
7. Stir at regular intervals while the pot is cooking.
8. When the rice has soaked most of the water, reduce the heat to low and cover the pot.
9. Allow to steam until completely done.
10. Serve alongside meat or fish.

Ready in about: 35 minutes, Servings: 3-4

Macaroni and Cheese

Macaroni and Cheese

Ingredients

- 1lb. elbow macaroni
- ½ cup butter
- 2 bags (about 16 oz) cheddar cheese
- ½ large green bell pepper, chopped
- ½ large white onion, chopped
- 4 medium-size eggs
- Black pepper to taste
- Salt to taste
- 2 tsp. paprika
- ½ scotch bonnet pepper, chopped finely
- ¾ cup evaporated milk

Instructions

1. Prepare the macaroni according to the packet direction.
2. Set the pot over medium heat and add the butter; heat until melted.
3. Strain the macaroni and add to the pot. Slowly and evenly incorporate the majority of the cheese. Reserve 8 ounces (or half of a 16-ounce bag) for later topping.
4. Combine the onion, paprika, black pepper, bell pepper, and scotch bonnet pepper. Stir until the cheese has melted and the mixture is smooth.
5. Gently beat the eggs and then fold them into the mixture.
6. Add evaporated milk slowly, stir thoroughly, and spread the batter evenly in a large prepared baking pan (about 13 x 9 inches).
7. Top with remaining cheese and loosely cover with foil.
8. Bake for approximately 1 hour at 375°F until the top is golden brown.
9. Allow 45-50 minutes for the macaroni to cool to room temperature before serving.

Ready in about: 1 hour 40 minutes, Servings: 6

Potato Salad

Potato Salad

Ingredients

- 6 medium white potatoes, quartered
- 1 tbsp. white vinegar
- 2 celery stalks, diced
- 3 green onions, finely sliced
- 4 hard-boiled eggs, peeled
- 1½ cups mayonnaise
- 1 tbsp. yellow mustard
- Salt to taste
- ¾ tsp. freshly ground black pepper
- Paprika flakes for garnish

Instructions

1. Bring a pot of water to a boil, then add the potatoes. Reduce the heat to a low boil and add salt to taste. Cook for about 20 minutes or until a fork or paring knife easily pierces the potatoes. Drain and place in a cool, dry place until cool enough to handle.
2. Potatoes should then be peeled and chopped. Transfer the potatoes to a large ceramic bowl and season with salt and pepper. Toss the potatoes with the vinegar and leave aside for 15-20 minutes to cool.
3. Add the celery and green onions to the potato combination. Add 4 finely chopped hard-boiled eggs to the potato mixture.
4. Combine the mayonnaise and yellow mustard in a bowl—season with salt and pepper to taste. Fold into the potato mixture.
5. If desired, sprinkle with paprika.
6. Before serving, chill for at least 1 hour or overnight.

Ready in about: 40 minutes, Servings: 8

Cracked Conch

Cracked Conch

Ingredients

- 3 pieces conch, per person
- Flour for dusting
- 1 egg
- 3 tbsp milk
- 1 cup oil for frying
- Salt and pepper to taste

Instructions

1. Beat the pieces of conch with a meat tenderizer on both sides.
2. Season with salt and pepper to taste.
3. Whisk the egg and milk together.
4. Dip the tenderized conch in the egg batter and then coat with the flour.
5. Deep fry in oil over medium heat until brown.
6. Serve with hot sauce and ketchup.

Ready in about: 40 minutes, Servings: 8

Crab Fat and Dough

Crab Fat and Dough

Ingredients

- 4 crabs
- 1 tbsp garlic powder
- 1 tbsp thyme
- 1 cup flour
- 1 tsp salt
- 1 tsp pepper
- 2 limes
- 1 tsp baking powder
- 3 tbsp softened butter
- Water to knead the dough
- Beer

Instructions

1. Remove the crab legs and discard.
2. Under the running water, clean the body of the crabs and the biters.
3. Squeeze the juice of 2 limes over the crabs.
4. Put the crabs in the pot, and then add enough beer that covers ¾ of the crabs. Add the salt, pepper, garlic powder, thyme, and boil the crabs.

Prepare the dough as follows:

5. In a bowl, combine the flour, salt, and baking powder.
6. Rub in the butter with your fingertips until thoroughly mixed, ensuring that there are no lumps. Add enough water to form a reasonably soft, flexible dough; knead until smooth.
7. Roll the dough flat until it reaches the circumference of the pot. Place the dough on the top of the crabs in the pot.
8. Cook for 25-30 minutes or until the dough rises and is firm to the touch. Serve the crabs and dough on a platter, ensuring that each person receives a crab body and the biters. Separate the crab and then dip the dough into the fat.

Ready in about: 50 minutes, Servings: 4

Grilled Lobster Tails

Grilled Lobster Tails

Ingredients

- 4 Lobster Tails – fresh or thawed
- 4 tbsp. softened butter
- 4 tbsp. fresh lemon juice
- Lemon pepper

Instructions

1. Preheat the grill to a medium-high temperature and lightly oil the grill.
2. With a sharp knife, cut the lobster tails in half lengthwise.
3. In a small bowl, combine the melted butter and lemon juice.
4. Brush the mixture onto the lobster tails' meat side.
5. Season with lemon pepper to taste.
6. Arrange the split lobster tails shell side down on the grill and cook for 3-4 minutes.
7. Flip the lobster tails and cook meat side down for another 3-4 minutes, taking care not to overcook.
8. Take the lobster off the heat, and brush with more melted butter and lemon pepper to taste.
9. Transfer to a serving dish and enjoy.

Ready in about: 20 minutes, Servings: 4

Fried Plantains

Fried Plantains

Ingredients

- 1-quart oil for frying
- 2 medium plantains

Instructions

1. Preheat oil over medium-high heat in a big, deep skillet.
2. Peel and chop the plantains in half.
3. Using a sharp knife, cut the halves lengthwise into thin slices.
4. Fry the pieces until they are golden brown on each side and soft. Do not burn.
5. Place absorbent paper towels on a plate.
6. Place the fried plantains on the plate to absorb the extra oil.
7. Serve with peas and rice.
8. Enjoy!

Ready in about: 15 minutes, Servings: 6

Coleslaw

Coleslaw

Ingredients

- 2 cups coleslaw mix (cabbage & carrots)
- ½ cup mayonnaise
- 2 tbsp. sugar
- 1½ tbsp. lemon juice
- 1 tbsp. White vinegar
- Salt and black pepper to taste

Instructions

1. Beat the mayonnaise, sugar, lemon juice, white vinegar, salt, and pepper in a large mixing bowl.
2. Stir in the coleslaw mix until everything is thoroughly combined.
3. Add more salt and pepper to taste as needed.
4. Refrigerate for a minimum of two hours before serving for the best flavour.
5. Enjoy!

Ready in about: 10 minutes, Servings: 4

Fire Engine (Corned Beef and White Rice)

Fire Engine (Corned Beef and White Rice)

Ingredients

- 1 tbsp. cooking oil
- 2 cans (12 oz each) corned beef
- 1 medium onion, finely chopped
- 1 small green bell pepper, finely chopped
- 1 stalk celery, finely chopped
- ¼ tsp. thyme
- 2 tbsp. tomato paste
- ¾ cup water
- Salt and black pepper to taste

Instructions

1. On medium-high heat, saute the onion, green bell pepper, and celery in a large frying pan with the oil until tender.
2. Add all the remaining ingredients into the frying pan, stirring regularly until the corned beef is heated through and becomes a smooth consistency.
3. Reduce the heat to low.
4. Cover the frying pan with a tight lid and cook for 10-15 minutes to ensure the ingredients sauté and flavours blend.
5. Serve with white rice.

Ready in about: 35 minutes, Servings: 3-4

Fried Snapper

Fried Snapper

Ingredients

- 1 egg, lightly beaten
- 1 cup flour
- 2 small limes for juice
- Salt and crushed bird pepper mixture
- 6 snappers
- 1/3 cup of milk
- Cooking oil for frying

Instructions

1. Cut slits into both sides of the snapper.
2. Season the fish on both sides with the salt and pepper mixture.
3. Squeeze the juice of two limes over it.
4. Let the fish marinate for 30 minutes.
5. Whisk the egg and one-third cup of milk together.
6. Dip the fish into the egg batter, then dust with flour on both sides.
7. Place the oil in a frying pan on medium heat until hot.
8. Deep fry the fish for five minutes on each side or until light golden brown.
9. Put absorbent paper towels on a plate.
10. Place the fried fish on the plate to allow the oil to be absorbed.
11. Serve right away.

Ready in about: 10 minutes, Servings: 6

Desserts

Guava Duff

Guava Duff

Ingredients

For Filling:
- 2 cups guava shells-seeded, peeled, and thinly chopped
- ¼ cup brown sugar
- ½ tbsp. Cinnamon powder
- ½ tsp. nutmeg
- 1 tbsp. butter
- 3 tbsp. water/rum/brandy

For Dough:
- 2 cups flour
- 2 tbsp. baking powder
- ¼ cup white sugar
- ½ cup melted butter
- 3 tbsp. milk
- 1 egg
- 2-3 tbsp. Water
- ½ tsp. salt

For Sauce:
- 1 cup Fresh Guava pulp
- 2 cups white icing sugar
- 2 tbsp. butter
- 2-tbsp rum
- 1 tsp lemon juice
- 1 tsp boiling water

Instructions

For Filling:
1. Set the pot over medium heat; add the chopped guava, water, sugar, cinnamon, butter, and nutmeg.
2. Cover the pot and bring it to a boil. Reduce to low heat and simmer until all the liquid has disappeared and the sugar has dissolved.
3. Transfer the filling to a bowl and set it aside to let cool.

For Dough:
4. Crack the egg and place it in a bowl—mix in the flour, baking powder, salt, sugar, and melted butter.
5. Then pour the milk slowly and combine well. If needed, then add water to it and knead the dough until it is firm and moist. Divide the dough in half and knead more until the dough looks soft and pillowy.
6. On a lightly floured board, roll out the dough like a jelly roll and spread some filling over the dough; roll the dough over the filling until the dough is swirled with filling.
7. Carefully seal all the edges. Wrap the dough in several layers of parchment paper, followed by two layers of foil. Fasten the two ends with a string and knot tightly—place in a big saucepan of boiling water and steam for one hour to set the duff.

For Sauce:
8. Combine the guava pulp, sugar, butter, rum, water, and lemon juice in a small bowl. Mix them well with a beater until the sugar dissolves, and the mixture is creamy and fluffy. Set aside in the fridge to chill.
9. Cut the guava duff loaf into 1-inch wide pieces and add a tablespoon of the sauce. Serve and enjoy the sweet duff.

Ready in about: 1 hour 45 minutes, Servings: 12-15

Guava Rum Cake

Guava Rum Cake

Ingredients

For Cake:
- ½ cup puree of fresh guava, strain seeds
- 2 tbsp. milk room temperature
- 4 large eggs
- 1 tsp. vanilla extract
- 2 tsp. coconut extract
- 2¼ cups cake flour sifted
- 1¾ cups white sugar
- 1 tbsp. baking powder
- 1 tsp. Salt
- ¾ tbsp. unsalted butter, softened (not melted)

For Rum Glaze:
- 1 cup puree of fresh guava (strain the seeds)
- ¾ cup dark rum
- 4 tbsp. water
- 1 cup sugar

Instructions

For Cake:
1. Preheat oven to 350 degrees and prepare a bundt pan as follows: spray the interior with floured baking spray (or use a grease/flour mixture).
2. Combine the puree, milk, eggs, and extracts in a small bowl and whisk until well combined. Add the sifted flour, baking powder, sugar, and salt to a stand mixer bowl.
3. Continue beating at a slow speed and gradually incorporate the butter. Combine until it is mixed and resembles moist crumbs.
4. Add the liquids and beat on medium speed for approximately 1 minute or blended entirely and evenly. Stop the mixer; wipe down the bowl sides, then mix by hand for an additional 30 seconds.
5. Transfer the batter to the pan.
6. Bake for approximately 25 minutes, or until a toothpick inserted in the centre emerges clean (time will vary). Let cake rest in the pan for nearly 10 minutes before turning out onto wire rack.
7. Allow cake to cool completely before serving (about 2 hours).

For Rum Glaze:
1. Puree the guava and remove the seeds using a filter.
2. Heat and mix the guava puree, sugar, water, and rum in a small pot. Stir and heat until the sugar has completely dissolved, and the mixture begins to boil. Thoroughly cool the sweetened guava purée.
3. Drop the rum glaze all over the cake. Serve and enjoy.

Ready in about: 1 hour + 2 hours to chill , Servings: 8

Coconut Tart

Coconut Tart

Ingredients

For Filling:
- 2 cups fresh coconut, shredded
- 1 cup white sugar
- 1 cup water
- ¼ tsp. nutmeg
- 1 tsp cinnamon
- 1 tsp. vanilla extract

For Dough:
- 1/3 cup of butter
- 1/2 cup white sugar
- 1/8 tsp of salt
- 1 instant packet yeast
- 4 1/4 cups flour
- 1 cup milk
- 1 egg beaten
- butter to brush the dough

Instructions

For coconut filling:
1. Set the small pot over medium heat and add the shredded coconut, sugar, water, nutmeg, cinnamon, and bring it to a boil.
2. Then reduce to low heat and continue cooking for nearly 5 minutes, or until the sugar has dissolved. Add the vanilla and mix.

For Dough:
3. Preheat the oven to 375 degrees F.
4. In a bowl, combine the sugar, salt and butter. Heat the milk and then add to the bowl stirring until the butter melts.
5. Combine the flour and yeast and add to the mixture. Then add the beaten egg.
6. Knead the dough for several minutes on a lightly floured board. Place the dough into a greased bowl and lightly grease the top of the dough.
7. Cover with a damp cloth.
8. When the dough has risen to twice its size, punch it and divide the dough in half. Make a smooth ball with each half and set it aside to rest for 10 minutes.
9. Roll out the rested dough into a rectangular shape and brush with melted butter. Put the coconut filling onto the dough and roll it up like a jelly roll, tuck in the ends.
10. Lay on a greased baking sheet and allow it to rise until double its size.
11. Bake for 25-30 minutes or until golden brown.

Ready in about: 2 hours 30 minutes, Servings: 8

Pineapple Tart

Pineapple Tart

Ingredients

For Filling:
- 1 tin of Crushed Pineapple
- 1 tbsp. Unsalted butter
- ½ cup white sugar
- ½ tsp. nutmeg
- 1/2 tsp. Vanilla

For Dough:
- 1/3 cup of butter
- 1/2 cup white sugar
- 1/8 tsp of salt
- 1 instant packet yeast
- 4 1/4 cups flour
- 1 cup milk
- 1 egg beaten
- butter to brush the dough

Instructions

Preparing Filling:
1. Set a pot over medium heat and add the butter.
2. Heat the butter until it has melted, then add the crushed pineapple and sugar.
3. Add the vanilla and nutmeg, and keep cooking until all the liquid has disappeared.

For Dough:
4. Preheat the oven to 375 degrees F.
5. In a bowl, combine the sugar, salt and butter. Heat the milk and then add to the bowl stirring until the butter melts.
6. Combine the flour and yeast and add to the mixture. Then add the beaten egg.
7. Knead the dough for several minutes on a lightly floured board. Place the dough into a greased bowl and lightly grease the top of the dough.
8. Cover with a damp cloth.
9. When the dough has risen to twice its size, punch it and divide the dough in half. Make a smooth ball with each half and set it aside to rest for 10 minutes.
10. Roll out the rested dough into a rectangular shape and brush with melted butter. Put the pineapple filling onto the dough and roll it up like a jelly roll, tuck in the ends.
11. Lay on a greased baking sheet and allow it to rise until double its size.
12. Bake for 25-30 minutes or until golden brown.

Ready in about: 2 hours 30 minutes, Servings: 8-10

Drinks

Sky Juice

Sky Juice

Ingredients

- 4 cups fresh coconut water
- ¼ cup coconut rum
- Condensed milk to taste
- Coconut jelly
- ¼ cup gin

Instructions

1. Into a jug, combine the coconut water with the gin and coconut rum.
2. Add the condensed milk to taste.
3. Next, add the coconut jelly.
4. Chill the drink mixture in the refrigerator for at least 2 hours.
5. Shake the mixture before pouring it into the serving glasses.
6. More gin and coconut rum may be added for a more robust flavour.
7. Enjoy!

Ready in about: 10 minutes, Servings: 4

Switcha Drink

Switcha Drink

Ingredients

- 1 cup fresh key lime juice
- 2 small lemons for juice
- 1 ½ cups white sugar
- 1-gallon water

Instructions

1. Put 1 1/2 cups of water in a pot on the stove.
2. Stir in the sugar until it is dissolved.
3. Bring the solution to a boil until it forms a simple syrup.
4. Combine the lime juice and lemon juice with the remaining water.
5. Ensure that there are no seeds by straining the mixture before placing it into a jug.
6. Add the simple syrup to the jug and stir well.
7. Refrigerate the juice for 30 to 60 minutes.
8. Serve with ice cubes.
9. Garnish the glass with a lime wedge.
10. Enjoy!

Ready in about: 1 hours 10 minutes, Servings: 4

Made in the USA
Columbia, SC
04 December 2023

27759671R00044